D1224967

Volume

Julie Murray

Abdo Kids Junior
is an Imprint of Abdo Kids
abdobooks.com

Abdo
MEASURE IT!
Kids

abdobooks.com

Published by Abdo Kids, a division of ABDO, P.O. Box 398166, Minneapolis, Minnesota 55439.

Printed in the United States of America, North Mankato, Minnesota.

052019

092019

Photo Credits: Alamy, iStock, Shutterstock

Production Contributors: Teddy Borth, Jennie Forsberg, Grace Hansen

Design Contributors: Christina Doffing, Candice Keimig, Dorothy Toth

Library of Congress Control Number: 2018963319

Publisher's Cataloging-in-Publication Data

Names: Murray, Julie, author.

Title: Volume / by Julie Murray.

Description: Minneapolis, Minnesota : Abdo Kids, 2020 | Series: Measure it! | Includes online resources and index.

Identifiers: ISBN 9781532185328 (lib. bdg.) | ISBN 9781532186301 (ebook) | ISBN 9781532186790 (Read-to-me ebook)

Subjects: LCSH: Volume (Cubic content)--Juvenile literature. | Thickness measurement--Juvenile literature. | Measurement--Juvenile literature.

Classification: DDC 530.813--dc23

Table of Contents

Volume

Volume is how much space something takes up.

500
400
200
5

We use many things

to measure volume.

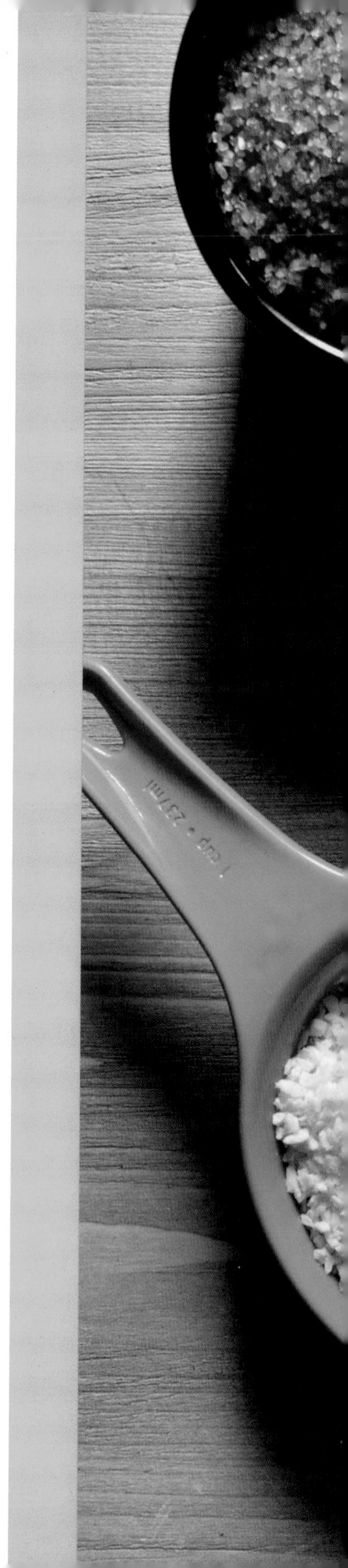

Lei makes soup. She adds a teaspoon of salt.

9

Mary is baking. She uses a tablespoon.

Zane makes pancakes.

He adds a cup of flour.

Mom is at the store. She buys a pint of ice cream.

Jenny loves strawberries.

She picks one quart.

Jane pours milk. It comes in a gallon jug.

Look around. We use volume to measure every day!

THIS OUT
THIS OUT

Let's Review!

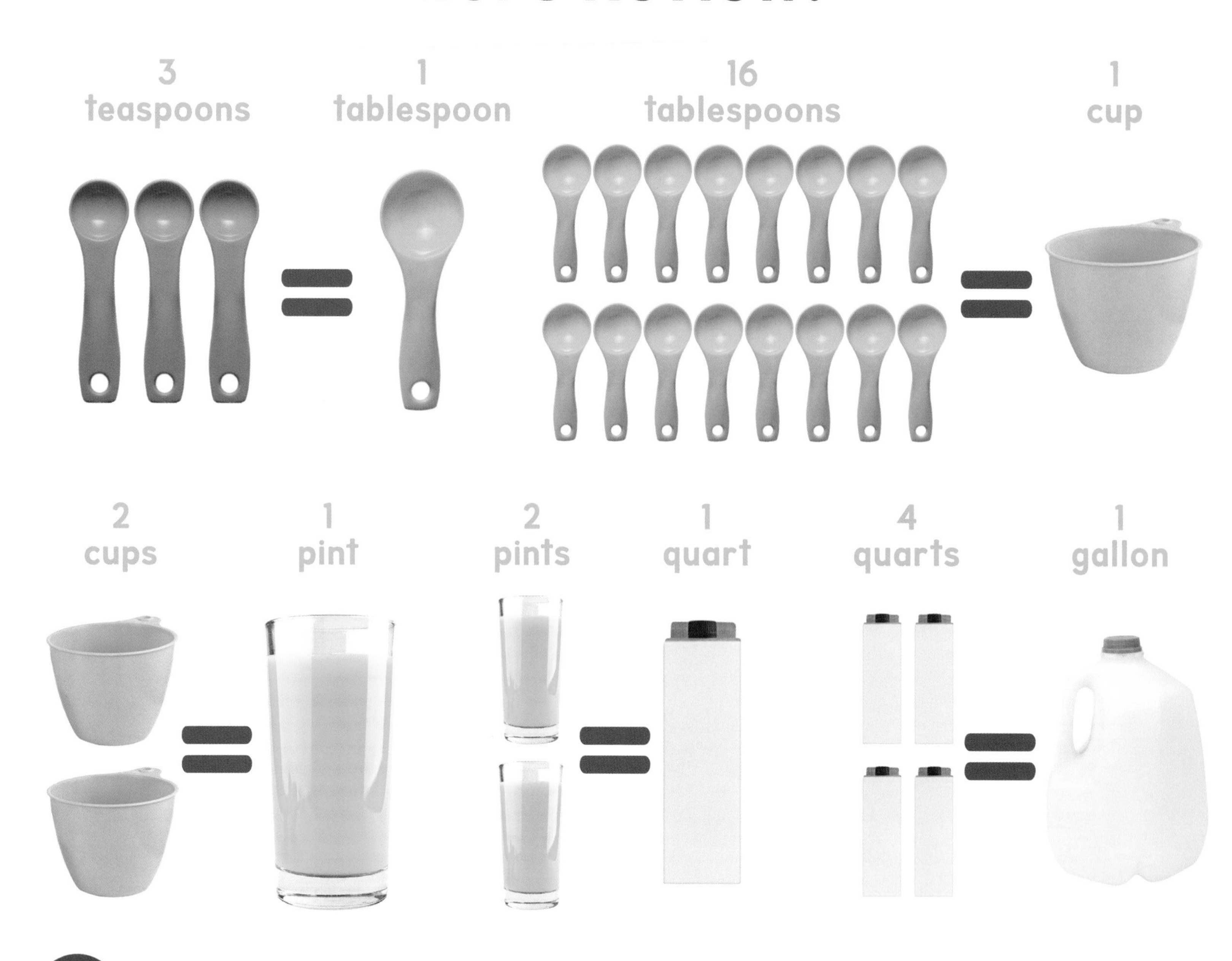

3
teaspoons
1
tablespoon
16
tablespoons
1
cup
2
cups
1
pint
2
pints
1
quart
4
quarts
1
gallon

Glossary

jug
a container for holding liquids. It often has a handle and an opening.

pour
to cause to flow in a steady stream.

Index

Visit **abdokids.com** to access crafts, games, videos, and more!

Use Abdo Kids code

MVK5328

or scan this QR code!